First World War
and Army of Occupation
War Diary
France, Belgium and Germany

16 DIVISION
Divisional Troops
Royal Army Medical Corps
Divisional Field Ambulance Workshop Unit
1 December 1915 - 31 March 1916

WO95/1968/1

The Naval & Military Press Ltd
www.nmarchive.com
Published in association with The National Archives

Published by

The Naval & Military Press Ltd

Unit 10 Ridgewood Industrial Park,

Uckfield, East Sussex,

TN22 5QE England

Tel: +44 (0) 1825 749494

www.naval-military-press.com

www.nmarchive.com

This diary has been reprinted in facsimile from the original. Any imperfections are inevitably reproduced and the quality may fall short of modern type and cartographic standards.

© **Crown Copyright**
Images reproduced by permission of The National Archives, London, England, 2015.

Contents

Document type	Place/Title	Date From	Date To
Heading	WO95/1968/1 16 Divn Divnl. Troops Divnl Field Amb. 1915 Dec-1916 Mar		
Heading	16th Division 16th Fd Amb. Workshop Unit Dec 1915-Mar 1916		
Heading	December 1915 Mar 16		
War Diary	Beaumetz-Les-Aires And Amettes	01/12/1915	01/12/1915
War Diary	Amettes	02/12/1915	31/12/1915
Heading	16th F.A.W.U. Vol.2 Jan 1916		
War Diary	Amettes.	01/01/1916	08/01/1916
War Diary	Auchy-Au-Bois	09/01/1916	31/01/1916
Heading	16th F.A.W.U. Feb 1916		
Heading	16th F.A.W.U. Vol.3 (Lau Lahore)		
War Diary	Auchy-Au-Bois	01/02/1916	27/02/1916
War Diary	Auchy-Au-Bois Busnes	28/02/1916	28/02/1916
War Diary	Busnes	29/02/1916	29/02/1916
Heading	16th F.A.W.U. Vol 4		
Heading	War Diary of 16th Divisional Field Ambulance-Workshop Unit, A.S.C. For The Month Of March 1916 Vol 4		
War Diary	Busnes	01/03/1916	08/03/1916
War Diary	Busnes And Lillers	09/03/1916	09/03/1916
War Diary	Lillers	10/03/1916	26/03/1916
War Diary	Lillers. Noeux	27/03/1916	27/03/1916
War Diary	Noeux	28/03/1916	31/03/1916

WO 95/1968/1

16 DIVN
DNNL. TROOPS
DIVNL. FIELD AMB. H/S DEC — 1916 MAR

16TH DIVISION

16TH FD AMB. WORKSHOP UNIT
DEC 1915 - MAR 1916

16TH DIVISION

16th F.A.W.U.
(late Lahore)
Vol I

D/7928

December 1915

Nov '16

Army Form. C. 2118

WAR DIARY
or
INTELLIGENCE SUMMARY

LAHORE Div.
F.A.N.U.
No. 46

(Erase heading not required.)

Instructions regarding War Diaries and Intelligence Summaries are contained in F.S. Regs., Part II. and the Staff Manual respectively. Title Pages will be prepared in manuscript.

Place	Date 1915	Hour	Summary of Events and Information	Remarks and references to Appendices
BEAUMETZ-LES-AIRES and AMETTES	Dec 1st		Total Strength 10 Officers, 68 N.C.Os and men, 1 Workshop, 1 Stove Waggon, 1 Stores Light Lorry, 23 Motor Ambulances, 1 Motor Car, 9 Motor Cycles. Unit moved under Brigade orders from BEAUMETZ-LES-AIRES at 9.30am and arrived at AMETTES at 10.50am. Pte Shaw S.A. (No. M2/033067) returned from leave and taken on the strength.	
AMETTES	Dec 2nd		Total Strength 10 Officers, 69 N.C.Os and men, 1 Workshop, 1 Stove Waggon, 1 Stores Light Lorry, 23 Motor Ambulances, 1 Motor Car, 9 Motor Cycles. General routine work in the workshop.	
AMETTES	Dec 3rd		Total Strength 10 Officers, 69 N.C.Os and men, 1 Workshop, 1 Stove Waggon, 1 Stores Light Lorry, 23 Motor Ambulances, 1 Motor Car, 9 Motor Cycles. Pte Streets J.R.J. (No. 102/823) admitted to Hospital. Strength of the Unit reduced in the workshop.	
AMETTES	Dec 4th		Total Strength 10 Officers, 68 N.C.Os and men, 1 Workshop, 1 Stove Waggon, 1 Stores Light Lorry, 23 Motor Ambulances, 1 Motor Car, 9 Motor Cycles, Pte Morgan E.R.G. (No. M2/4821) returned from leave taken on the strength. Pte Elkin R.V.E. (No. R.E.(9911) and Naick George Bedal were posted from the Unit and taken on the strength. General routine work in the workshop.	
AMETTES	Dec 5th		Total Strength 10 Officers, 73 N.C.O and men, 1 Workshop, 1 Stove Waggon, 1 Stores Light Lorry, 23 Motor Ambulances, 1 Motor Car, 9 Motor Cycles. Pte Boyle H (No. M2/073502) returned from leave and taken on the strength. General routine work in the workshop.	

Army Form. C. 2118

WAR DIARY
or
INTELLIGENCE SUMMARY
(Erase heading not required.)

LAHORE Div. Field Ambulance Workshop Unit

No. 47

Place	Date 1915	Hour	Summary of Events and Information	Remarks and references to Appendices
AMETTES	Dec 1		Total Strength 1 Officer, 7 N.C.O. and men, 1 Workshop Motor Waggon, 1 Motor light van, 23 Motor Ambulances, 1 Motor car, 9 Motor cycle, 6 cycles. Cpl. Fisher, G.J. (No M2/105970) returned from leave and taken on the Strength. General nature of work as usual.	
AMETTES	Dec 4		Total Strength 1 Officer, 75 N.C.O. and men, 1 Workshop Motor Waggon, 1 Motor light van, 23 Motor Ambulances, 1 Motor car, 9 Motor cycle, 6 cycles. 2850 drawn for Remittance Roll from Field Cashier. Pte Constable, R. (No. 3622). Admitted 2 days for ineff. R.W.R. 978 to absence from duty. Pte Dunnill, G. (No M2/115186) admitted to Hospital sickness syphilis.	
AMETTES	Dec 8		Total Strength 1 Officer, 74 N.C.O. and men, 1 Workshop Motor Waggon, 1 Motor light van, 23 Motor Ambulances, 1 Motor car, 9 Motor cycle, 6 cycles. Paid out N.C.O's and men 2630 francs.	
AMETTES	Dec 9		Total Strength 1 Officer, 74 N.C.O. and men, 1 Workshop Motor Waggon, 1 Motor light van, 23 Motor Ambulances, 1 Motor car, 9 Motor cycle, 6 cycles. Returned to Police supply column Motor cycle No. 93506 and received Motor cycle No. 95444. Motor Ambulance No. A1466 came in with damaged worm wheel. Total Strength 1 Officer, 74 N.C.O. and men, 1 Workshop, 1 Motor Waggon, 1 Motor light van, 23 Motor Ambulances, 1 Motor car, 9 Motor cycle, 6 cycles. On instructions from the D.D.S.T. 1st Army No. ST9139, dated 7/XII/15 to	

WAR DIARY
or
INTELLIGENCE SUMMARY

Army Form. C. 2118

LAHORE Div.
F.A.W.U.

No. 48

Place	Date	Hour	Summary of Events and Information	Remarks and references to Appendices
AMETTES	Dec 10th		Headquarters, Indian Cav. Southern Touring Car No. M14732 exchanged with the Ind. Div. F.A.W.U. for Daimler Car No. M1289, the latter being received in a very dirty and worn in condition. General nature of work in the workshop. Pte Gunning, 14 No. M.S. 3642, awarded due to Southern Field Punishment No. 2 for neglecting orders.	
AMETTES	Dec 11th		Total strength 10 Officers, 74 N.C.O.s and men, 1 Stores Wagon, 1 Store Wagon Motor Lorries, 2 Motor Cycles, 9 M.S.W. Cycles, 2 N.C.O.s and 25 men of No. 23 M.S.W. Ambulance, 1 M.S.W. Box Car. Workshop after the entraining of No. 111 S.F.A. working on Daimler Car No. M1289 in front axle.	
AMETTES	Dec 12th		Total strength 10 Officers, 74 N.C.O.s and men, 1 Stores Wagon, 1 Store Wagon Motor Lorries, 23 M.S.W. Ambulance, 1 M.S.W. Box Car, 9 M.S.W. Cycles. General nature of work in the workshop.	
AMETTES	Dec 13th		Total strength 10 Officers, 74 N.C.O.s and men, 1 Stores Wagon, 1 Stores Wagon, with No. 7 B.F.A., No. 8 B.F.A., No. 112 S.F.A., and No. 113 S.F.A. Left 9 sound vans of No. 23 M.S.W. Ambulance, 1 M.S.W. Cav. M.S.W. Ambulance attended. Workshop after entraining of Field Ambulance. Several nature work in the workshop. Pte Worrell E. (9-M2/115669) returned from hospital and taken on the strength. General nature work in the workshop.	

Army Form. C. 2118

WAR DIARY
or
INTELLIGENCE SUMMARY
(Erase heading not required.)

LAHORE Div. FF.W.W.

N° 49

Place	Date 1915	Hour	Summary of Events and Information	Remarks and references to Appendices
AMETTES	Dec 14th		Total Strength 10 Officers, 75 N.C.Os and men, 1 Workshop, 1 Store Waggon, 1 Stores Light Lorry, 23 Ambulances, 9 Motor Cycles, 1 Motor Car. Under instruction from D.O.T. (N°8696) Ambulances Motor Ambulances N° A14731, A14728, A14663, A14662, A14661 and A14730 with 12 personnel were this day transferred to the 1st Indian Cavalry Division, this unit receiving in exchange Ambulance M.T. Ambulances N° M1553, M1554, M1547, M1549, M1614 and M1551, with 12 personnel.	
AMETTES	Dec 15th		Total Strength 10 Officers, 75 N.C.Os and men, 1 Workshop, 1 Stores Light Lorry, 23 Ambulances, 9 Motor Cycles, 1 Motor Car. Under instruction from D.O.T. (N°8696) Siddeley Deasy Motor Ambulances N° A14659, A14721, A14658, A14720, A14660, and Daimler Motor Ambulances N° A9299, A14251, A17430, A17434 with 16 personnel were this day transferred to the 2nd Indian Cavalry Division and in exchange were received to the ambulances sent yesterday an Ambulance M.T. Ambulance N° M1864.	
AMETTES	Dec 16th		Total Strength 10 Officers, 59 N.C.Os and men, 1 Workshop, 1 Stores Waggon, 1 Stores Light Lorry, 14 Ambulances, 9 Motor Cycles, 1 Motor Car. Received from the Supply Column of the 1st Army Troops Supply Column Ambulance N° M1864. Under instruction from D.O.T. (N°8696) Vauxhall Motor Ambulances N° M1865, M1867, M1852, M1862, M1856 with nine personnel N° A.F.A.115 transferred to 86th Div F.A.W.U. in which we received from them in exchange Ambulance Motor Ambulance N° A178. Motor Ambulances received today in exchange were found to be on inspection in a very dirty neglected and uncared for condition.	
AMETTES	Dec 17th		Total Strength 10 Officers, 68 N.C.Os and men, 1 Workshop, 1 Stores Waggon, 1 Stores Light Lorry, 20 Ambulances, 9 Motor Cycles, 1 Motor Car. Condition of ambulances recently received general overhaul of ambulance recently received.	

Army Form. C. 2118

WAR DIARY
or
INTELLIGENCE SUMMARY
(Erase heading not required.)

LAHORE Div FFAvU No SD

Place	Date	Hour	Summary of Events and Information	Remarks and references to Appendices
AMETTES	19.6.18		Trial through 18 Officers 68 NCOs and men 1 Workshop, 1 Store Waggon 1 Stores yet any 20 Ambulances 9 Motor cycles, 1 Motor car. General nature work in the workshop.	
AMETTES	19.6.19		Total through 10 Officers 68 NCOs and men 1 workshop, 1 Store Waggon, 1 Stores yet any 20 Ambulances 9 Motor cycles, 1 Motor car. General nature work in the workshop	
AMETTES	19.6.20		Total through 10 Officers 68 NCOs and men 1 Workshop, 1 Store Waggon, 1 Stores yet any 20 Ambulances 9 Motor cycles, 1 Motor car. General nature work in the workshop	
AMETTES	19.6.21		Total through 10 Officers 68 NCOs and men 1 Workshop, 1 Store Waggon, 1 Stores yet any 20 Ambulances 9 Motor cycles, 1 Motor car. General nature work in the workshop. Received into G.H.Q. Repair Shop M.T.284, Lorry Bus No. M1284. Received into G.H.Q. Repair Shop with M.D/109247.	
AMETTES	19.6.22		All Clerkwagon W.B. and struck off the strength of the day. Sent 3 no han Total strength 10 Officers 67 NCOs and men, 1 Workshop, 1 Store Waggon, 1 Stores yet any 20 Ambulances, 9 Motor cycles.	
AMETTES	19.6.23		Total through 10 Officers 67 NCOs and men, 1 Workshop, 1 Store Waggon, 1 Stores yet any 20 Ambulances, 9 Motor cycles. General nature work in the workshop.	
AMETTES	19.6.24		Total through 10 Officers 67 NCOs and men, 1 Workshop, 1 Store Waggon, 1 Stores yet any 20 Ambulances, 9 Motor cycles. Trade Waggon (No. M2/0882) and Ghreits C. (No. M2/0657) transferred to Corps yd. with tray and to Lillin A (No. M2/0189416) transferred to base 6 Divnl. General nature work in workshop	
AMETTES	19.6.25		Total through 10 Officers 67 NCOs and men 1 workshop 1 stores yet any Light Lorry 20 Ambulance 9 Motor cycles, 8c Bee, 1 Car M2/093758 given eight days Field Punishment No. 2 for committing an act to the prejudice of good order and military discipline. Received return Instructions to report to the XVIth Divnal area that your today the	

Army Form. C. 2118

WAR DIARY
or
INTELLIGENCE SUMMARY
(Erase heading not required.)

N⁰ 57   XVIᵀᴴ Divisional F.A.W.U.

Place	Date 1915	Hour	Summary of Events and Information	Remarks and references to Appendices
AMETTES	Dec 26		Name of the unit is "XVIᵀᴴ Divisional F.A.W.U." General routine work in the workshop.	
AMETTES	Dec 26		Total Strength 10 Officers, 67 N.C.O. and men, 1 Workshop, 1 Stores lorry, 1 Store light lorry, 20 Ambulances, 9 Motor cycles, 7 Motor Ambulances and tenders. Personnel reported for duty with N⁰ 112 Field Ambulance and 5 Motor Ambulance and Motor Ambulance personnel reported for duty with N⁰ 113 Field Ambulance. General routine work in the workshop.	
AMETTES	Dec 27		Total Strength 10 Officers, 67 N.C.O. and men, 1 Workshop, 1 Store lorry, 1 Stores light lorry, 20 Ambulances, 9 Motor cycles, 2 Motor cycles detailed for duty at circles and ambulance of N⁰ 111 and N⁰ 112 F.A. General routine work in the workshop.	
AMETTES	Dec 28		Total Strength 10 Officers, 67 N.C.O.s and men, 1 Workshop, 1 Stores lorry, 1 Store light lorry, 20 Ambulances, 9 Motor cycles. General routine work in the workshop.	
AMETTES	Dec 29		Total Strength 10 Officers, 67 N.C.O. and men, 1 Workshop, 1 Stores light lorry, 20 Ambulances, 9 Motor cycles. General routine work in the workshop.	
AMETTES	Dec 30		Total Strength 10 Officers, 67 N.C.O. and men, 1 Workshop, 1 Stores lorry, 1 Stores light lorry, 20 Ambulances, 1 Motor Ambulance detailed to duty with N⁰ 112 F.A., 9 Motor cycles. General routine work in the workshop.	
AMETTES	Dec 31		Total Strength 10 Officers, 67 N.C.O. and men, 1 Workshop, 1 Stores lorry, 1 Stores light lorry, 20 Ambulances, 9 Motor cycles, 1 Motor Ambulance detailed to duty with N⁰ 112 F.A. This makes the complement of N⁰ 112 F.A. up to taking complete. L H. C.
O. XVIᵀᴴ Divisional F.A.W.U.	

16th Faw.V.
Vol. 2

Jan 1916

Army Form. C. 2118

WAR DIARY
or
INTELLIGENCE SUMMARY
(Erase heading not required.)

XVIth Divisional F.A.W.U

No. 5

Place	Date 1916	Hour	Summary of Events and Information	Remarks and references to Appendices
AMETTES	Jan 1		Total Strength 10 Offrs, 67 N.C.O and men, 1 workshop, 1 Pk Waggon, 1 Stores Lge, Horse Lge, Army, 20 Ambulance, 9 M/Pr Cycls. General nature of work in the workshop.	
AMETTES	Jan 2		Total Strength 10 Offrs, 67 N.C.O and men, 1 workshop, 1 Pk Waggon, 1 Stores Lge, Army 20 Ambulance, 9 M/Pr Cycls, Sundale Single Car Brand Army No 1477 attached to Headquarters brought into workshop, badly damaged. General nature of work in the workshop.	
AMETTES	Jan 3		Total Strength 10 Offrs 67 N.C.O and men, 1 Workshop, 1 Pk Waggon, 1 Stores Lge, Army 20 Ambulance, 9 M/Pr Cycls. Ambulance M/Pr Ambulance No A1786 with 6pdr Gear RVE (NRE/8811) received from the 21st Lancers Cavalry Division and taken in for through overhauling. Car No 1777. General nature work.	
AMETTES	Jan 4		Total Strength 10 Offrs 68 N.C.O and men, 1 Workshop, 1 Store Waggon, 1 Stores Lge, Army, 21 Ambulance, 9 M/Pr Cycls. General nature work in the Workshop.	
AMETTES	Jan 5		Total Strength 10 Offrs, 68 N.C.O and men, 1 Workshop, 1 Stores Waggon, 1 Stores Lge, Army, 21 Ambulance, 9 M/Pr Cycls. Car No 1777 Returned to Headquarters after completion of repairs.	
AMETTES	Jan 6		Total Strength 10 Offrs 68 N.C.O and men, 1 Workshop, 1 Stores Waggon, 1 Stores Lge, Army, 21 Ambulance, 9 M/Pr Cycls. Ambulance No A1786 brought into Workshop daily and reported in general overhauling daily and regular condition.	

WAR DIARY
or
INTELLIGENCE SUMMARY

XVTH DIVISIONAL F.A.W.U.

No. 52

Place	Date	Hour	Summary of Events and Information	Remarks and references to Appendices
AMETTES	June 6		Under instruction from D.A.Q, G.H.Q. 3rd Echelon, Petts No. 4/90/107 of 11/5/915, Cpl Glen R.V.E. (No R.E. 9811) sent to Other Command of Reinforcements, MARSEILLES. General nature work in Workshop.	
AMETTES	June 7		Total strength 10 Officers, 67 NCO and men, 1 workshop, 1 stores wagon, 1 store wagon. No. 21 Ambulance, 9 Motor cycles. 3 Motor cycles No. 254 + 94, 255622 and 254470 returned to the Supply Column, the exchanges for new ones having off the strength. General nature work in the Workshop.	
AMETTES	June 8		Total strength 10 Officers, 67 NCO and men, 1 workshop, 1 store wagon, 1 store wagon. No. 21 Ambulance, 6 Motor cycles. 1 Workshop car No. M15548, attached to the Divisional Train turned into the Workshop with having her collision with a cart, and badly damaged. Same to be Workshop Mechanised was notified from Divisional Headquarters & AUCHY-AU-BOIS, the Motorman A. (No. R597w) Brown J.H (No. M2/054942) Payne R (No. 12475) Wham J.E. (No. M2/113634) and Rice W.A. (No. DM2/117625) joined the unit and taken on the strength.	
AUCHY-AU-BOIS	June 9		Total strength 10 Officers, 72 NCO and men, 1 Workshop, 1 Store wagon, 1 Store wagon, No. 21 Ambulance, 6 Motor cycles. 1 Workshop in Workshop.	
AUCHY-AU-BOIS	June 10		Total strength 10 Officers, 72 NCO and men, 1 Workshop, 1 Store wagon, 1 Store wagon, No. 21 Ambulance, 6 Motor cycles.	
AUCHY-AU-BOIS	June 11		Total strength 10 Officers, 72 NCO and men, 1 Workshop, 1 Store wagon, 1 Store wagon, No. 21 Ambulance, 6 Motor cycle 9 E. Roberts E. (No. PM L4350) granted the work leave and struck off the strength. General nature work being in collision. No. 20733.	

WAR DIARY or INTELLIGENCE SUMMARY

Army Form. C. 2118

No. 53

XVI74 Divisional
F.F.W.U.

Place	Date 1916	Hour	Summary of Events and Information	Remarks and references to Appendices
AUCHY-AU-BOIS	Jany 12th		1 Slice through 1 Officer, 7 N.C.O. and men, 1 Wt/Sergt, 1 Store Wagon, 1 Water Cart, 1 Ambce any, 21 Ambulance, 6 M/Cu cycles, entraining Grunch Lury No 209.	33
AUCHY-AU-BOIS	Jany 13th		Total through 1 Officer, 7 N.C.O. & men, 1 Sergeant, 1 Store Wagon, 1 Water Cart of any 21 Ambulance, 6 M/Cu Cycles. Entrain M/Cu Ambulance No F.U 666. With Punch Recorders & (M.A. 5936 and M.A. 5956) and Speed T. (M2/020 127) forwd. veh 2138 to M.T. Pk C.G. HQ WK Loste twn wheel and stud (Off be Wagons	
AUCHY-AU-BOIS	Jany 14th		Total through 1 Officer 10 this 69 NCO and men, 1 Sergeant, 1 store wagon, 1 water cart, 1 any 20 Ambulance, 6 M/Cu Cycles. General motor work in the Workshops. Strip 2 Leu Krupps tour tube bodies to Forgetshame Pell Workshop on Divisional Train Ambulance M/Cu Ear No M 15542	
AUCHY-AU-BOIS	Jany 15th		Total through 10 this 69 NCO and men, 1 workshop, 1 Store Wagon, 1 Ecn Cycle, 1 any 20 Ambulance 6 M/Cu Cycle. 1 Cft. Lorrd E.G. (No M2/10396) and Pte. Wilson (No M2/098938) mounted & taking Livedsgood and No 24402mr in Forgetshame Poll and tour to form to Porvels.	
AUCHY-AU-BOIS	Jany 16th		Total through 1 Officer 69 NCO and men, 1 workshop, 1 Store Wagon, 1 Mfs Cycle, 1 any 20 Ambulance 6 M/Cu Cycle. Working in Ironwood Train Ambulance Ear No.	
AUCHY-AU-BOIS	Jany 17th		Total through 10 this 69 NCO and men 1 workshop 1 Store wagon, 1 Mfs cycle, 1 any 20 Ambulance, 6 M/Cu Cycle. Working in Ironwood Ear No M/5547	

Army Form. C. 2118

WAR DIARY
or
INTELLIGENCE SUMMARY

(Erase heading not required.)

16th Divisional
F.A.W.U.

J. - 94

Place	Date	Hour	Summary of Events and Information	Remarks and references to Appendices
AUCHY-AU-BOIS	Jany 18		Total Strength 10 Officers, 69 NCO and men, 1 Workshop, 1 Steve Wagon, 1 Box Lyst, 1 my, 20 Ambulances, 6 Motor Cycles. Under instruction from the D.A.G., G.H.Q. 3rd Echelon dated 14/1/16 No: 3378 9 privates Youell F (No M2/077084) Mitchinson A (No R 5974) Payne D (No M2/2187), Evans P (No M2/077084) (No 19 M2/117625) and Blackburn A (No M2/020126) returned to Base M.T. Depot ROUEN. M/S Patterson E (No M2/098767) granted eight days leave and temporarily struck off the strength. 4 Ford Ambulance No: RGb 67 handed in w/r lasting Line Instr. Order	
AUCHY-AU-BOIS	Jany 19		Total Strength 10 Officers, 61 NCO and men, 1 workshop, 1 Steve Wagon, 1 Box Lyst, 1 my, 20 Ambulances, 6 Motor Cycles. Lys. Driver on Ford Ambulance No: A 9647. General routine work in the workshop. Private Martin (No M2/020632) and one P. (No M2/020862) granted one weeks leave and temporarily struck off the strength.	
AUCHY-AU-BOIS	Jany 20		Total Strength 10 Officers, 59 NCO and men, 1 Workshop, 1 Steve Wagon, 1 Box Lyst, 1 my, 20 Ambulances, 6 Motor Cycles. Ford Ambulance Car No: 1977 having at times inadequate work faulty magneto armature and returned to Divisional Supply Received Workshop Ford Car No: M 11272 to replace same.	
AUCHY-AU-BOIS	Jany 21		Total Strength 10 Officers, 59 NCO and men, 1 Workshop, 1 Steve Wagon, 1 Box Lyst, 1 my, 20 Ambulances, 6 Motor Cycles, 1 M.C. Car Received from the Divisional Supply Column 3 singles, M.C. Cycle, No: 19008 1782 and 1991. General routine work in the workshop.	
AUCHY-AU-BOIS	Jany 22		Total Strength 10 Officers, 59 NCO and men, 1 Workshop, 1 Steve Wagon, 1 Box Lyst, 1 my, 20 Ambulances, 9 Motor Cycles, 1 Motor Car & Cars. L (No M3/4350)	

WAR DIARY or INTELLIGENCE SUMMARY

Army Form. C. 2118

XVIth DIVISION/FL
FA.WU
N[o] 55

Place	Date	Hour	Summary of Events and Information	Remarks and references to Appendices
AUCHY-AU-BOIS	Jany 22	10//	returned from leave and taken on the strength. Total strength 10 officers, 60 N.C.O. and men, 1 workshop, 1 store waggon, 1 box car, 2 G. (N[o] M2/050931) and taken on the strength. Granted one week's leave and temporary duty on the workshop.	
AUCHY-AU-BOIS	Jany 23		Total strength 10 officers, 60 N.C.O. and men, 1 workshop, 1 store waggon, 1 light van 21 Ambulance, 9 motor cycles, 1 motor car. Received ambulance N[o] F.13338 for Reinstatement Roll. Under instructions from D.A.D.M.S., G.H.Q. 3rd Echelon dated 14/1/1916 (N[o] 3375) Pte Meads, J.A. (N[o] M2/032 dog) sent to Base M.T. Depot and struck off the strength. General routine work in the workshop.	(N[o]M2/032620)
AUCHY-AU-BOIS	Jany 24		Total strength 10 officers, 59 N.C.O. and men, 1 workshop, 1 store waggon, 1 van, 21 Ambulance, 9 motor cycles, 1 motor car. Working on alterations to Ford Ambulance and general routine work.	
AUCHY-AU-BOIS	Jany 25		Total strength 10 officers, 59 N.C.O. and men, 1 workshop, 1 store waggon, 1 van, 21 Ambulance, 9 motor cycles, 1 motor car. Working on alterations to Ford Ambulance and general routine work. Pte Inman, A. (N[o]M2/104849) granted one week's leave and temporary duty on the workshop.	
AUCHY-AU-BOIS	Jany 26		Total strength 10 officers, 58 N.C.O. and men, 1 workshop, 1 store waggon, 1 van, 1 light Ford Ambulance, 9 motor cycles, 1 motor car. Working on alterations to Ford Ambulance and general routine work in the workshop. M[c]Pattern, J. (N[o]M2/08917) returned from leave and taken on the strength.	
AUCHY-AU-BOIS	Jany 27		Total strength 10 officers, 59 N.C.O. and men, 1 workshop, 1 store waggon, 1 light van, 21 Ambulance, 9 motor cycles, 1 motor car. Pte Smith T.H. (N[o]M2/08873) granted one week's leave and temporarily struck off the strength.	

Army Form. C. 2118

WAR DIARY
or
INTELLIGENCE SUMMARY   XVIIth Divisional
No. 56   F.A.W.U

(Erase heading not required.)

Instructions regarding War Diaries and Intelligence Summaries are contained in F.S. Regs., Part II. and the Staff Manual respectively. Title Pages will be prepared in manuscript.

Place	Date	Hour	Summary of Events and Information	Remarks and references to Appendices
Auchy-au-Bois	Jany 29		Total Strength 10 Officers 58 N.C.O. and men, 1 workshop, 1 Store waggon, 21 Ambulances, 9 M/Cr cycles, 1 M/Cr Cn, 9h P.C. Richards, 1 (No 129/018/20) granted one weeks leave and temporarily joined 9th the strength 9th Malta J (N° M2/020/032) and 1 are J (N° M2/020/982) returned from leave and taken on the strength. Working in attachment to Field Ambulance, and general nature work.	
Auchy-au-Bois	Jany 30		Total Strength 10 Officers 58 N.C.O. and men, 1 workshop, 1 Stores waggon, 1 Cars, Light Lorry, 21 Ambulances, 9 M/Cr cycles, 1 M/Cr Car, Pte. Tutterton T (N° 6487) joined the unit and taken on the strength. General nature work in the workshop.	
Auchy-au-Bois	Jany 31		Total Strength 10 Officers 60 N.C.O. and men, 1 workshop, 1 Store waggon, 1 Cars, Light Lorry, 21 Ambulances, 9 M/Cr cycles, 1 M/Cr Car. Working in attachment to Field Ambulance, and general nature work.	

J.P. Stibbon
Lt-C. S.C.
O.C. XVIIth Div. F.A.W.U

16th Jawn.

Feb 1916

16th 7. A. W. U.
Vol: 3
(Late Lahore)

WAR DIARY or INTELLIGENCE SUMMARY

Army Form. C. 2118

WITH 1ST Div. EA WU

N° 57

Place	Date	Hour	Summary of Events and Information	Remarks and references to Appendices
AUCHY-AU-BOIS	Feb 1		Total Strength 1 Officer 60 N.C.O. and men 1 Workshop, 1 Horse Wagon, 1 Horse light Lorry, 21 Ambulance, 9 Motor Cycles, 1 Motor Car. Working on absorption to Ford Ambulance, and general routine work in the Workshop.	
AUCHY-AU-BOIS	Feb 2		Total Strength 1 Officer 60 N.C.O. and men 1 Workshop, 1 Horse Wagon, 1 Horse light Lorry, 21 Ambulance, 9 Motor Cycles, 1 Motor Car. Private Evans A.T. (N°M2/020970) and Driver E. (P.M2/920898) proceeded on leave and temporarily struck off the strength. General routine work in the Workshop.	
AUCHY-AU-BOIS	Feb 3		Total Strength 1 Officer 58 N.C.O. and men 1 Workshop, 1 Horse Wagon, 1 Horse light Lorry, 21 Ambulance, 9 Motor Cycle, 1 Motor Car Pte Clark E. (N°M2/104360) proceeded on leave and temporarily struck off the strength. Pte Johnson A. (N°M2/104849) returned from leave and temporarily taken on the strength. General routine work in the Workshop.	
AUCHY-AU-BOIS	Feb 4		Total Strength 1 Officer 58 N.C.O. and men 1 Workshop, 1 Horse Wagon, 1 Horse light Lorry, 21 Ambulance, 9 Motor Cycle, 1 Motor Car Pte Smart T.H. (N°M2/018973) returned from leave and taken on the strength. Returned to Ford Ambulance and general routine work in the Workshop.	
AUCHY-AU-BOIS	Feb 5		Total Strength 1 Officer 59 N.C.O. and men 1 Workshop, 1 Horse Wagon, 1 Horse light Lorry, 21 Ambulance, 9 Motor Cycle, 1 Motor Car. L/Cpl Hale L. (N°M2/02288) granted leave and temporarily struck off the strength. Lurlcan Motor Ambulance N° M1662 towed into Workshop with broken crown wheel. Returned to Ford Ambulance.	
AUCHY-AU-BOIS	Feb 6		Total Strength 1 Officer 58 N.C.O. and men 1 Workshop, 1 Horse Wagon, 1 Horse Lorry, 21 Ambulance, 9 Motor Cycle. Pte Richards J. (N°M2/048620)	

WAR DIARY or INTELLIGENCE SUMMARY

XVI Corps F.A.W.L.
No. 58

Place	Date	Hour	Summary of Events and Information	Remarks and references to Appendices
AUCHY-AU-BOIS	Feb 3/6		Returned from leave and taken on the strength. Pte Elliott T. (N° M2/2625) returned from leave and taken on the strength. Resuming Divisional Field Kitchens and general routine work.	
AUCHY-AU-BOIS	Feb 4/6		Total strength 1 Officer, 60 ON CO and men. 1 Workshop, 1 Stove Wagon, 1 Store Wagon, 2 Ambulances, 9 M.Tr Cycles, 1 M.Tr Cars. Pte Elliott T. (N° M2/2625) forfeited under Sec. 138 (a) Army Act 12/10 days to make good such compensation for service received by him in that whilst on leave to ENGLAND losing his return ticket allowed to the R.T.O. return station for a return warrant. N° 39/160 (Table N° 4258). General routine work in the workshop.	
			Total strength 1 Officer, 60 ON CO and men. 1 Workshop, 1 Stove Wagon, 1 Store Wagon, 2 Ambulances, 9 M.Tr Cycles. Pte Elliott T. (N° M2/2625) awarded 7 days Field Punishment N°2, under Sec. 40 (5) Army Act for absence without leave in that he, which on leave to England, absented himself from duty in hour away after expiration of the date of his return. Driver M Tn Ambulance N° M1662 WK Pte Bur. T.S. (N° M2/050937) Transferred to 356 Co GHQ M.T. M.T. With broken arm whilst acting small SF he through. Pte Elliott T. (N° M2/2625) admitted to Hospital School of the through. Pte Bunglam J. (N° M2/022175) Granted leave to England through England General routine work in the Workshop.	
AUCHY-AU-BOIS	Feb 5/6		Total strength 1 Officer, 59 NCO and men. 1 Workshop, 1 Store Wagon, 1 Stove Wagon, 2 Ambulances, 9 M.Tr Cycles, 1 M.Tr Car. A/Cpl Walker (N° M2/103526) Granted 14 days leave and temporarily struck off the strength. General Routine work in the workshop.	

Army Form. C. 2118

WAR DIARY or INTELLIGENCE SUMMARY

(Erase heading not required.)

Army Form C. 2118

XVITH DIVISIONAL F.A.W.U.

No. 59

Place	Date	Hour	Summary of Events and Information	Remarks and references to Appendices
Auchy-au-Bois	Feb 10		Total Strength 1 Officer, 5 N.C.O. and men, 1 Workshop, 1 Horse Waggon, 1 Horse Light Lorry, 20 Ambulances, 9 Motor Cycles, 1 Motor Car. Pte. Lynn H. (N°M2/098796) granted one weeks leave and temporary struck off the Strength. General routine work in the Workshop. Private Evans A.T. (N°M2/020970) and Orme E. (N°M2/020898) returned from leave and taken on the Strength.	
Auchy-au-Bois	Feb 11		Total Strength 1 Officer, 57 N.C.O. and men, 1 Workshop, 1 Horse Waggon, 1 Horse Light Lorry, 20 Ambulances, 9 Motor Cycles, 9 Motor Cycles, 1 Motor Car. Steps from Field Cashier 3000 francs in Regimental Pay and 300 Francs in advance of Pte Clark. R.E. (N°M2/104360) returned from leave and taken on the Strength	
Auchy-au-Bois	Feb 12		Total Strength 1 Officer, 58 N.C.O. and men, 1 Workshop, 1 Horse Waggon, 1 Horse Light Lorry, 20 Ambulances, 9 Motor Cycles, 1 Motor Car. Pte Piniel nil of 58 N.C.O. and men 2975 francs and forward Acquittance Roll 60 book 6 (N°M2/100557) granted one weeks leave and temporarily struck off the Strength. General routine work in the Workshop.	
Auchy-au-Bois	Feb 13		Total Strength 1 Officer, 57 N.C.O. and men, 1 Workshop, 1 Horse Waggon, 1 Horse Light Lorry, 20 Ambulances, 9 Motor Cycles, 1 Motor Car. Pte. Mayle W. (N°M2/022188) returned from leave and taken on the Strength. General routine work in the Workshop.	
Auchy-au-Bois	Feb 14		Total Strength 1 Officer, 58 N.C.O. and men, 1 Workshop, 1 Horse Waggon, 1 Horse Light Lorry, 20 Ambulances, 9 Motor Cycles, 1 Motor Car. Pte. Hawkins T.S. (N°M2/10735) joined the Unit and taken on the Strength. General routine work in the Workshop.	
Auchy-au-Bois	Feb 15		Total Strength 1 Officer, 59 N.C.O. and men, 1 Workshop, 1 Horse Waggon, 1 Horse Light Lorry, 20 Ambulances, 9 Motor Cycles, 1 Motor Car. Pte Lockwood G.W. (N°M2/098788)	

WAR DIARY
or
INTELLIGENCE SUMMARY   XVIth Div. F.A.N.U.

Army Form. C. 2118

No. 00.

Place	Date	Hour	Summary of Events and Information	Remarks and references to Appendices
AUCHY-AU-BOIS	Feby 15 1916		Granted one weeks leave to England and temporarily struck off the strength. General routine work in the workshop.	
AUCHY-AU-BOIS	Feby 16		Total strength 10 officers 58 N.C.O and men 1 workshop, stores waggon, stores lorry 1 and 20 Ambulances. 9 M/cles 1 cycle 1 M/cle car Ambulance B/Pte Providence No A17846 brought into workshop with broken down wheel. General routine work in the workshop.	
AUCHY-AU-BOIS	Feby 17		Total Strength 10 Officers 58 N.C.O and men 1 workshop, stores waggon, stores lorry 1 and 20 Ambulances, 9 M/cles 1 cycle, 1 M/cle car. Privates McMunn J (No M2/102195), Keen A (No M2/019219), McDonald I (No M2/077442), Keast A (No M2/033067) and Futerman L (No M2/040727) granted leave to England and temporarily struck off the strength. Sunbeam M/cle Ambulance No A17246 inuneated to 358 Co. F.S. MT 44Q. Lieut. Pte Brown J.H. (No M2/051492) and struck off the strength. General routine work in the workshop.	
AUCHY-AU-BOIS	Feby 18		Total Strength 10 Officers 58 N.C.O and men 1 workshop, stores waggon, stores lorry 1 19 Ambulances 9 M/cles 1 cycle, 1 Motor car. Lt-Col Burton W (No M2/09575) and Private Taylor J (No M2/019230) granted leave to England and temporarily struck off the strength. Pte Taylor G.H. (No M2/10273) joined the unit from the Base M.T. Depot and taken on the strength. A/Cpl. Wakely E.J. (No M2/103326) and Private England J (No M2/022145) returned from leave taken on the strength.	
AUCHY-AU-BOIS	Feby 19		Total Strength 10 Officers 58 N.C.O and men 1 workshop, stores waggon stores lorry 1 19 Ambulances, 9 M/cles 1 cycle, 1 M/cle car. Private Finlay R.J. (No M2/135601) and Sergeant H (No 15 M2/134644) with Ford M/cle Ambulance No A9966 joined the	

Army Form. C. 2118

WAR DIARY
or
INTELLIGENCE SUMMARY

(Erase heading not required.)

XVIII Div. 54th Bn.

Instructions regarding War Diaries and Intelligence Summaries are contained in F.S. Regs., Part II. and the Staff Manual respectively. Title Pages will be prepared in manuscript.

Place	Date	Hour	Summary of Events and Information	Remarks and references to Appendices
AUCHY-AU-BOIS	Feb 19		Unit arrived & taken on the strength. Pte Bell H (SP M2/098765) granted one privilege leave and equivalents stand off the strength. General nature work in the locality.	
AUCHY-AU-BOIS	Feb 20		Total strength 18 Officers, 54 NCO and men, 1 workshop, 1 steam lorry, 1 steam lorry (light), 20 Ambulances, 9 M/Cy cycle, 9 M/Cr cycles, 1 M/Cr cars, 1 M/Cr car. Pte Patton G.G. (19 M2/115269) granted one weeks leave to England and equivalents stand off the strength. General nature work within the locality.	
AUCHY-AU-BOIS	Feb 21		Total strength 18 Officers, 53 NCO and men, 1 workshop, 1 steam lorry, 1 steam lorry (light), 20 Ambulances, 9 M/Cr cycle, 1 M/Cr car. Pte Wilson S.J. (19 M2/098753) granted one weeks leave to England and stand off the strength. Cpl Shears G.H. (19 M2/098310) promoted to Sergeant with pay, No.113 Field Ambulance. General nature work in the locality.	
AUCHY-AU-BOIS	Feb 22		Total strength 18 Officers, 52 NCO and men, 1 workshop, 1 steam lorry, 1 steam lorry (light), 20 Ambulances, 9 M/Cr cycle, 1 M/Cr car. Pte Thompson E. (19 M2/101457) granted one weeks leave and equivalents stand off the strength. General nature work within the locality.	
AUCHY-AU-BOIS	Feb 23		Total strength 18 Officers, 51 NCO and men, 1 workshop, 1 steam lorry, 1 steam lorry (light), 20 Ambulances, 9 M/Cr cycle, 20 Ambulances, 1 M/Cr car. Pte Shears G (19? 08.13?) returned from leave and taken on the strength. Driver M.T. Dyson A. struck off the strength to unknown destination. General nature work within the locality.	
AUCHY-AU-BOIS	Feb 24		Total strength 18 Officers, 51 NCO and men, 1 workshop, 1 steam lorry, 1 steam lorry (light), 20 Ambulances, 9 M/Cr cycle, 1 M/Cr car. General nature work and forwarded Registration Roll dated 1st Feb 2050 Years NCO and men and forwarded Registration Roll	

Army Form. C. 2118

WAR DIARY
or
INTELLIGENCE SUMMARY

(Erase heading not required.)

XVIIth Div. FAWU

N° 6?

Place	Date	Hour	Summary of Events and Information	Remarks and references to Appendices
AUCHY-AU-BOIS	Feby 25		Total strength 1 Officer, 57 N.C.O. and men, 1 workshop, 1 Spt. wagon, 1 Stores wagon, 1 M. Cr. Cycle, 20 Ambulances, 1 M. Cr. Ambulance. N° A.8791 Pvt. Smalls Bevan S. (N° M2/078932) agnd. Ambs. W(N° M2/078484) joined the unit and taken on the strength. General natures work in the workshop. Pte. (N° M2/078932) Pvt. Harvey P. (N° M2/078782) Sent Army $? (N° M2/078700) Pvt. Ray H. (N° M2/078932) leave ? (N° M2/078782) returned. Pte. Jolly H. & Cor. Hockney (N° M2/078782) granted leave to England and proceeded through.	
AUCHY-AU-BOIS	Feby 26		Total strength 1 Officer, 4 N.C.O. and men, 1 workshop, 1 Spt. wagon, 1 Stores wagon, 1 M. Cr. Cycle, 21 Ambulance, 1 M. Cr. Ambulance. Mtr. Ambulance N° 1864 with Pvte. Dunn E. (N° M2/020898) and Evans A.T. (N° M2/020970) evacuated £358 6a Pte. M.T. G.H.Q. Park carried out petrol and Oil consumption. He strength General nature work in the workshop. Received officer instructions from G.H.Q. to move the unit on the 28th instant to the vicinity of BUSNES.	
AUCHY-AU-BOIS	Feby 27		Total strength 10 Officer, 47 N.C.O. and men, 1 workshop, 1 Spt. wagon, 1 Stores wagon, 1 M. Cr. Cycle, 20 Ambulance, 1 M. Cr. Ambulance. Pte. Lakenham & Logg. Long. Q. M. Cr. Cycle & Pte. (N° M2/046727) returned from leave and taken on the strength. Loading lorries & ready for moving. Pte. Reen. F. (N° 121/019209) returned from leave taken on the strength, who is to M. C. on. S. M. (N° M2/02145).	
AUCHY-AU-BOIS BUSNES	Feby 28		Total strength 1 Officer, 50 N.C.O. and men, 1 workshop, 1 Stores wagon, 1 Spt. wagon, 1 M. Cr. Cycle. 1 M. Cr. Amb. Unit left AUCHY-AU-BOIS for BUSNES at 9.45 am arriving at 11 am Capt Beck (N° M2/078785) and Pte. Sandal (N° M2/07442) returned from leave and taken on the strength. Unloading and general natures work in the workshop.	
BUSNES	Feby 29		Total strength 1 Officer, 53 N.C.O. and men, 1 workshop, 1 Spt. wagon, 1 Stores wagon, 1 M. Cr. Cycle, 1 M. Cr. Amb. General natures work in the workshop. Pte. Potter G. M. G.	

Army Form. C. 2118

WAR DIARY
or
INTELLIGENCE SUMMARY XVI TH Div. FA. W.U.

(Erase heading not required.)

No. 63

Instructions regarding War Diaries and Intelligence Summaries are contained in F. S. Regs., Part II. and the Staff Manual respectively. Title Pages will be prepared in manuscript.

Place	Date	Hour	Summary of Events and Information	Remarks and references to Appendices
BUSNES	Feb 29 1916		(N.M.2/1568a) and Motor T.L (N.M.2/019230) returned from leave and taken on the strength. Reinforcements to Ford M.T. Car Ambulances	

J.T. Watson
O.C. XVI Th Div. FA. W.U.

LRG

16th F.A.W.U.
Vol: 4

WAR DIARY

of

16th Divisional Field Ambulance - Workshop Unit, A.S.C.

FOR THE MONTH OF MARCH 1916

VOL. I

COMMITTEE FOR THE
MEDICAL HISTORY OF THE WAR

Date   9- JUN.1916

Army Form. C. 2118

WAR DIARY
or
INTELLIGENCE SUMMARY

N° 64   XVII.In.F.A.M.U.

(Erase heading not required.)

Instructions regarding War Diaries and Intelligence Summaries are contained in F. S. Regs., Part II. and the Staff Manual respectively. Title Pages will be prepared in manuscript.

Place	Date	Hour	Summary of Events and Information	Remarks and references to Appendices
BUSNES	Feb 1st 1916		Total strength 10 Officers 55 N.C.O. & and men 1 workshop & stores lorry 20 Ambulance, 9 Motor bycycles. 1 Midnight Lorry A.A. (N° M/2/033070) returned from leave.	
BUSNES	Feb 2		Total strength 10 Officers 52 N.C.O. and men. 1 workshop & stores lorry 20 Ambulance, 9 M.C. cycles. 1 Motor cycle. 1 Private Lorry general nature work returned to Private Miller.	
BUSNES	Feb 3		Total strength 10 Officers 56 N.C.O. and men. 1 workshop & stores lorry 20 Ambulance, 9 M.C. cycles. 1 Motor lorry. Private Gregory, Private Light. The Units and taken on the strength. Pte. Smith L. (N° M/2/100557) and Pte Gregory J. general nature work. E. (N° M/2/101457) returned from leave and taken on the strength. Publication Miller.	
BUSNES	Feb 4		Total strength 10 Officers 58 N.C.O. and men 1 workshop & stores lorry 20 Ambulance, 9 Motor cycles. 1 Motor car. Pte. Gregory J. Stone Light given three months furlough. M/2/2217. Pte. Baldwin R.C. (N° M/2/109074) through (workshop to Mechanical Transport Depot) and responding to all the motor vehicles. Transferred to base N° M 4597 turned into workshop with Private Baldwin sore. 1 working.	
BUSNES	Feb 5		Total strength 10 Officers 58 N.C.O. and men 1 workshop & stores lorry 20 Ambulance, 9 Motor cycles. 1 Motor car. A. Cpl. Wilson J. (N° M/2/098758) returned from leave and taken on the strength. Pte. Elliott J. (N° M/2/26525) and alterations to Ford Ambulance. Pte. Elliott T. (N° M/2/121/25) admitted to No. 138(4) Field Amb. ill as in the strength 21-13-0 P.M. Long request made good time returned to unit. Compensation for injuries caused by Germans while on Privates leave in Regent St Glasgow on February 3rd 1916.	

No. 36 Howard St. Euston, LONDON.

WAR DIARY
or
INTELLIGENCE SUMMARY XVIIth Div FA___

Army Form. C. 2118

Place	Date	Hour	Summary of Events and Information	Remarks and references to Appendices
BUSNES	M.5.16		Lt Elliot T(R.M.A) (3/3/45) answered sick. Major Fuller relinquished P.O in neglect of returning orders confirming. In structions to O.C.R. M4347 received. Attention to Fred Mobile Ambulance	
BUSNES	M.6.		Total strength 10Officers 60NCO and men 1workshop 1stores lorry lorry 20 Ambulances, 9Motor Cycles, 1Motor bus @M2/078760) Station @(SUR M2/078952) Trace Y(RM2/077678) and Harvey P(RM2/078783) returned from leave and taken on the strength. General routine work in the workshops.	
BUSNES	M.7.		Total strength 10Officers 64NCO and men 1workshop 1stores lorry lorry 20 Ambulances, 9Motor Cycles, 1Motor bus General routine work in the workshops. Received orders to move workshop unit to LILLERS on the strength.	
BUSNES	M.8.		Total strength 10Officers 64NCO and men 1workshop 1stores lorry lorry 20 Ambulances, 9Motor Cycles, 1Motor bus General routine work in workshop.	
BUSNES and LILLERS	M.9.		Total strength 10Officers 64NCO and men 1workshop 1stores lorry lorry 20 Ambulances, 9Motor Cycles, 1Motor bus On Motor unit from BUSNES at 11:30am arriving at LILLERS at 12:30 pm. Unloading Unit and general routine work in the workshops.	
LILLERS BUSNES	M.10.		Total strength 10Officers 64NCO and men 1workshop 1stores lorry lorry 20 Ambulances, 9Motor Cycles, 1Motor bus On Outstanding First Mobile Ambulance	
LILLERS	M.11.		N° A9967 Total strength 10Officers 64NCO and men 1workshop 1stores lorry lorry 20 Ambulances, 9Motor Cycles, 1Motor bus Sent from Field Establ stores lorry to Reparature Pool. General routine work in the workshops.	

WAR DIARY or INTELLIGENCE SUMMARY

Army Form. C. 2118

No. 10   1 E. J.N. F.A.N.U

Place	Date 1916	Hour	Summary of Events and Information	Remarks and references to Appendices
LILLERS	Mch 11		Jo Jackling T.B. (O.R.M.) (0135) admitted to Hospital and temporarily struck off strength. Total through 10 Offrs 13 NCO and men 11 Officers 1 Star Baggage Wag 1 Box Lorry 20 Ambulance 9 Motor Cycles 1 Motor Lorry and no 9790 Estate W.N.C. 6 and men	
LILLERS	Mch 12		and General Registrar's Role. General service wgn. Total through 10 Offrs 13 NCO and men 1 Lorry 1 Box Baggage Wag 1 Box lorry 20 Ambulance 9 Motor Cycles 1 Motor Car. Two JNC by the LP 25 and 2247/2 (0121+681) returned to H.Q. of General Supply Column and struck off the strength	
LILLERS	Mch 13		Total through 13 Offrs 63 NCO and men Motorised 1 box baggage 1 box lorry 20 Ambulance 9 Motor Cycles 1 Motor Car. 1 Motor Ambulance No. 9791 brought into workshop with damaged axle struck off as course being lately taken over at workshop	
LILLERS	Mch 14		Total through 10 Offrs 63 NCO and men 3 Lorries 1 Staff car 20 Ambulance 9 Motor Cycles 1 Motor Car. At 1300 telegram No. RZ/B-38 stated M3/9761 to be struck off. At 1830 BD. NH. YHR wrote an ambulance for the King's Office the baggage has been taken out (N9 NM3/9791) strength. Working in Motor Ambulance No. 9791	
LILLERS	Mch 16		Total through 13 Offrs 63 NCO and men 1 box baggage 1 box lorry 20 Ambulance 1 Motor cycles 1 Motor car	
LILLERS	Mch 17		Total through 10 Offrs 63 NCO and men 1 Box lorry 1 box baggage 20 Ambulance 1 Motor cycles 1 Motor car. Motor Ambulance N°9791 having been repaired and returned with an ambulance. Has broken down which broke into workshop with broken down wheel	

Army Form. C. 2118

WAR DIARY
or
INTELLIGENCE SUMMARY

(Erase heading not required.)

No. 67 16 & 17 F.W.U.

Instructions regarding War Diaries and Intelligence Summaries are contained in F. S. Regs., Part II. and the Staff Manual respectively. Title Pages will be prepared in manuscript.

Place	Date	Hour	Summary of Events and Information	Remarks and references to Appendices
LILLERS	Mar 18		Total strength 1 Officer, 8 N.C.O. and men. Workshop Store, Wagon Store, Light Lorry, 20 Ambulances, 1 Motor Cycle, 1 Motor Car. Officer Commanding B.E. (No M2/07449) Sergt. E (No M2/09878) and Graham E (No M2/10575) sent to the Base M.T. Depot (Reference R.O. Convoy No 2 dated 15th February 1916. Workshop on Motor Ambulance No 1867 which was returned to section in day.	
LILLERS	Mar 19		Total strength 1 Officer, 59 N.C.O and men. Workshop Store, Wagon Store, Light Lorry, 20 Ambulances, 7 Motor Cycle, 1 Motor Car. Private Douglas, Motor Cycle No 23359 and 22509 from the 16th Div Supply Column and taken on strength. Pte Harding T.J. (No. M/10635) returned from Hospital and taken on strength. General motor work in the workshop.	
LILLERS	Mar 20		Total strength 1 Officer, 59 N.C.O and men. Workshop Store, Wagon Store, Light Lorry, 20 Ambulances, 9 Motor Cycle, 1 Motor Car. M2/09788. Pte Johnson E.G. promoted to Corporal with rank as from March 15th 1916. General motor work in the workshop.	
LILLERS	Mar 21		Total strength 1 Officer, 60 N.C.O. and men. Workshop Store, Wagon Store, Light Lorry, 20 Ambulances, 9 Motor Cycle, 1 Motor Car, 1 Indian Motor Car. Ambulance No A995 with Pte Good W.G. (No M2/04593W) for me the last this day taken in the Workshop. General motor work in the workshop.	
LILLERS	Mar 22		Total strength 1 Officer, 61 N.C.O and men. Workshop Store Wagon Store Light Lorry, 21 Ambulance, 9 Motor Cycle, 1 Motor Car. G.H. Sergt G.H. (No. M2/019310) granted six weeks leave to England and subsequently struck off the strength. New from him Lister 2500 fitter for Regimental Duty.	
LILLERS	Mar 23		Total strength 1 Officer, 60 N.C.O and men. Workshop Store, Wagon Store, Light Lorry, 21 Ambulance, 9 Motor Cycle, 1 Motor Car. General motor work in the workshop.	

WAR DIARY or INTELLIGENCE SUMMARY

Army Form. C. 2118

No. 16 16th J in F.A.N.U.

Place	Date 1916	Hour	Summary of Events and Information	Remarks and references to Appendices
LILLERS	Mar 23		Received orders from the A.D.M.S. to move Infantry Unit from LILLERS to NOEUX in the 20th Division. 9 T.U., 6 R.A.M.C. and 3 R.E. men temporarily attached to Unit from today. Total strength 10 Offrs, 60 NCO and men. 1 Workshop stores Wagon, Stores Wagon, Water Cart — 2 Ambulance, 9 Motor Cycles, 1 Lorry with 1 NCO and men. 355 horses and Forward Reparation Park. General nature work on the Workshop.	
LILLERS	Mar 25		Total strength 10 Offrs, 60 NCO and men, 1 Workshop, 1 Store Wagon, Stores Wagon 2 Ambulance, 9 Motor Cycles, 1 Lorry. Died in June, A(N°73) 628935, Gunner Winnifred Plank. Transferred to No. 13 F.A. at 2 hours 40 mins and struck off the strength. General nature work in the Workshop.	
LILLERS	Mar 26		Total strength 10 Offrs, 60 NCO and men, 1 Workshop, 1 Store Wagon, Store Wagon, 2 Ambulance, 9 Motor Cycles, 1 Lorry. Today's work in the Workshop. G.R.O. 446 Battery Workshop Section under ORE hydraulic Entrunk work in the Workshop.	
LILLERS & NOEUX	Mar 27		Total strength 10 Offrs, 60 NCO and men, 1 Workshop, 1 Store Wagon, Store Wagon, 2 Ambulance, 9 Motor Cycles, 1 Lorry. Unit moved from LILLERS to NOEUX and arrived at NOEUX at 10.30 P.M. at 8.35 P.M.	
LILLERS NOEUX	Mar 28		Total strength 10 Offrs, 60 NCO and men. 1 Workshop, 1 Store Wagon, Stores Wagon, 2 Ambulance, 9 Motor Cycles, 1 M/Cycle. Evacuated to Original Depot No. 14397 L 2nd R.F.C. Pyrein Pilet No. ROUEN to end. General nature work in the Workshop.	
NOEUX	Mar 24		Total strength 10 Offrs, 60 NCO and men. 1 Workshop, 1 Store Wagon, Store, 2 Ambulance, 9 Motor Cycles, 1 M/Cycle. 1 Offr. departed on 14 days leave to ENGLAND and Temporarily struck off the strength. No. (A/T) 1290765 Spr. General nature work in the Workshop.	

WAR DIARY
or
INTELLIGENCE SUMMARY

(Erase heading not required.)

Army Form. C. 2118

No. 69 1/4 In. F.A.N.U.

Place	Date	Hour	Summary of Events and Information	Remarks and references to Appendices
NOEUX	Mch 30 1916		Total strength 10 offrs. 54 N.C.O. & men. 1 workshop & stores lorry, Motor light lorry, 2 Ambulances, 9 Motor cycles, 1 Motor car. General nature of the day's work.	
NOEUX	Mch 31		Total strength 10 offrs. 54 N.C.O. and men. 1 workshop & stores lorry, Motor light lorry, 2 Ambulances, 9 Motor cycles, 1 Motor car. General nature of work in the workshop.	

E.J. Walker
O.C. 16 In. F.A.N.U.

L.992

www.ingramcontent.com/pod-product-compliance
Lightning Source LLC
Chambersburg PA
CBHW081501160426
43193CB00013B/2553